Air F

The complete beginner's guide to easy and delicious recipes, smart people on a budget for quick and easy meals.

LAURA OWEN

Introduction

Air fryers are fundamentally scaled-down ledge convection ovens with a heating component over the food and a solid fan. As it creates heat, the fan circles the sight-seeing to enable the food to cook equitably and crispy. When contrasted with customary rotisserie foods, most air fried food surfaces have fundamentally the same as smash without utilizing a huge amount of oil or fat. Truth be told, we scarcely need to utilize any oil and the food despite everything that turns out crispy and scrumptious. Most food likewise turns out like it's flawlessly roasted in a convection oven with magnificent roasted flavors and surfaces. When breaded and splashed with oil, food becomes crunchy and fundamentally the same as what you would cook in a profound fryer.

We needed to tell everybody that air broiling isn't about re-heating solidified comfort foods. Indeed, it's incredible for heating remains and cooking snappy solidified bites. You can cook crisp, healthy, and healthy recipes in the air fryer. No doubt. Try not to JUDGE. Truly, we made a decision from the start, yet after our first straightforward feast for two individuals in under 20 minutes, we were snared and fixated and wild. Consequently, the formation of overly new and delightful recipes for the cookbooks.

Low-Fat Meals: Unarguably, the most basic advantage of the air fryer is its utilization of sight-seeing circulation to prepare nourishment fixings from all edges, in this manner wiping out the requirement for oil use. This makes it workable for individuals on a low-fat eating regimen to serenely prepare brilliantly sound suppers.

More beneficial Foods & Environment: Air fryers are intended to work without swelling oils and to deliver more advantageous nourishments with up to 80 percent less fat. This makes it simpler to get in shape since you can at present eat your seared dishes while moderating the calories and soaked fat. Doing that change to a more advantageous life is increasingly reachable by utilizing this apparatus. Your house is additionally freed of the fragrance that accompanies Pan-fried nourishments that regularly remains around the climate even a few hours after profound broiling.

Multipurpose Use: The air fryer empowers you to perform various tasks as it can prepare numerous dishes on the double. It is yours across the board machine that can flame broil, heat, fry, and meal those dishes that you love! You never again need numerous apparatuses for different occupations. It can do different employments separate machines will do. It can barbecue meat, cook veggies, and heat baked goods. It fills in as a viable substitution for your broiler, profound fryer, and stovetop.

Incredibly Safe: Remember how extra cautious you must be while tossing chicken or some different fixings into the profound fryer? You need to guarantee that the hot oil doesn't spill and consume your skin since it's in every case extremely hot. With your air fryer, you wouldn't have to stress over brunt skin from hot oil spillage. It does all the broiling and is protected. By the by, use cooking gloves while repositioning your fryer to maintain a strategic distance from dangers from the warmth.

Furthermore, keep your air fryer out of youngsters' compass.

Simple Clean Up: The Air Fryer leaves no oil and, along these lines, no wreckage. Tidy up time is agreeable since their oils spill to clean on dividers and floors, and no rejecting or scouring of the container. The Air fryer parts are made of non-stick material, which keeps nourishment from adhering to surfaces along these lines, making it difficult to clean. These parts are anything but difficult to clean and keep up. They are removable and dishwasher-sheltered too.

Spare Valuable Time: People who are on tight calendars can utilize the quickness of the air fryer to make tasty suppers. For occasions, you can make French fries in under 15 minutes and heat a cake inside 25 minutes. Inside minutes as well, you can appreciate fresh chicken fingers or brilliant fries. On the off chance that you are consistently in a hurry, the air fryer is perfect for you since you will invest less energy in the kitchen. It empowers you to deal with your rushed and occupied day by day life, filling your heart with joy increasingly sensible.

Prepare your fixings and put them into the crate, and afterward set your clock. The tourist goes to work, and when his work is finished, the clock goes off with a ding sound, showing that your nourishment is finished. You may even check your nourishment to perceive how it's advancing without upsetting the set time. When you pull out the container, the fryer will delay; when you place back the skillet, warming will proceed.

The Air fryer is a direct apparatus, with no collecting required and no confusion. It comprises three principle things; the cooking container, the skillet, and the primary fryer unit.

The Cooking Basket is the place you put your nourishment. It has a crate handle where you place your hand when taking care of the apparatus and prepared nourishment to forestall consumption or wounds when the air fryer is turned on. The bushel fits splendidly into the skillet. The pan gathers the nourishment remainders and overabundance oil and fits impeccably into the air fryer & then we have The Main Fryer Unit, which comprises numerous parts. Other helpful parts incorporate a rack, twofold flame broil layer, a bushel, and nourishment separators that make it conceivable to prepare various dishes immediately.

Contents

CHAPTER 1: WHAT IS AN AIR FRYER?

An air fryer utilizes the convection mechanism in cooking food. It circulates hot air through the use of a mechanical fan to cook the ingredients inside the fryer.

The process was named after the person who first explained it in 1912, French chemist Louis-Camille Maillard. The effect gives a distinctive flavor to browned foods, such as bread, biscuits, cookies, pan-fried meat, seared steaks, and many more.

The air fryer requires only a thin layer of oil for the ingredients to cook. It circulates hot air up to 392 degrees Fahrenheit. It's an innovative way of eliminating up to 80 percent of the oil that is traditionally used for frying different foods and preparing pastries.

You can find a dose of friendly features in air fryers, depending on the brand you're using. Most brands include a timer adjustment and temperature control setting to make cooking easier and precise. An air fryer comes with a cooking basket where you'll place the food. The basket is placed on top of a drip tray. Depending on the model you're using, you will either be prompted to shake the basket to distribute the oil evenly, or it automatically does the job via a food agitator.

This is perfect for home use, but if you're cooking for many people and you want to apply the same cooking technique, you can put your food items in specialized air crisper trays and cook them using a convection oven. An air fryer and convection oven apply the same technique in cooking, but an air fryer has a smaller built and produces less heat.

Directions Use Your Air Fryer

This appliance comes with a manual for easy assembly and as a handy guide for first-time users. Most brands also include a pamphlet of recipes to give your ideas about the wide range of dishes that you can create using this single kitchen appliance. Once you are ready to cook and you have all your ingredients ready, put them in the basket and insert them into the fryer. Other recipes will require you to preheat the air fryer before using it. Once the basket is in, set the temperature and timer and begin cooking.

You can use an air fryer for cooking food in a variety of ways. Once you get used to the basics, you can try its other features, such as advanced baking and using air fryer dehydrators.

Here are some of the cooking techniques that you can do with this single appliance:

Fry: You can omit oil in cooking, but a little amount adds crunch and flavor to your food. You can add oil to the ingredients while mixing or lightly spray the food with oil before cooking. You can use most kinds of oils, but many users prefer peanut, olive, sunflower, and canola oils.

Roast: You can produce the same quality of roasted foods as the ones cooked in a conventional roaster in a faster manner. This is recommended to people who need to come up with a special dish but do not have much time to prepare.

Bake: There are baking pans suited for this appliance that you can use to bake bread, cookies, and other pastries. It only takes around 15 to 30 minutes to get your baked goodies done.

Grill: It effectively grills your food easily and without a mess. You only need to shake the basket halfway through the cooking process or flip the ingredients once or twice, depending on the instructions. To make it easier, you can put the ingredients in a grill pan or grill layer with a handle, which other models include in the package, or you can also buy one as an added accessory.

There are many kinds of foods that you can cook using an air fryer, but there are also certain types that are not suited for it. Avoid cooking ingredients, which can be steamed, like beans and carrots. You also cannot fry foods covered in heavy batter in this appliance.

Aside from the above mentioned, you can cook most kinds of ingredients using an air fryer. You can use it for cooking foods covered in light flour or bread crumbs. You can cook a variety of vegetables in the appliance, such as cauliflower, asparagus, zucchini, kale, peppers, and corn on the cob. You can also use it for cooking frozen foods, and home-prepared meals by following a different set of instructions for these purposes.

An air fryer also comes with another useful feature - the separator. It allows you to cook multiple dishes at a time. Use the separator to divide ingredients in the pan or basket. You have to make sure that all ingredients have the same temperature setting so that everything will cook evenly at the same time.

Cleaning and maintenance of Air Fryer

Along with careful cleaning, an electric appliance also needs constant maintenance. To ensure personal safety, all the components of the product have to be checked at least once a week. It is important to examine the power cord and its functionality. In case of the following anomalies, contact the Instant pot support team immediately:

1. If the power plug and cord show any damage, deformation, discoloration, and expansion.

2. If a certain portion of the power plug and the cord feels hotter than usual.

3. If the instant pot shows abnormal heating or emits a burnt smell.

4. If the cooker produces any abnormal sounds or vibrations when its power is on.

Caution: Unplug the device immediately when you find any such anomalies. Do not try to repair anything by yourself. Contact the support team and discuss the issue in detail.

CHAPTER 2: BENEFITS OF THE AIR FRYER

Healthy cooking, time saver, easy of use, easy of clean up, versatility

Healthier Cooking: add an air fryer to your kitchen gadgets if you're looking to cut down on calories but don't want to lose flavor or taste. Although deep frying food can use up to three cups of oil, most air fryers use only one cubic cubicle. They use air and minimum oil to heat and cook the food. The effect is crispy meals with fewer calories than conventional deep frying.

Time-saving kitchen utensil: This takes some time to pre-heat oil and ovens. An air fryer can achieve a temperature in a matter of minutes. In an air fryer, food cooks quicker too.

Easy to use: Many air fryers come with presets to cook popular dishes by pressing a button. Because cooking is done within the air fryer, and the temperature is set automatically, walking away from it is healthy and not worried about grease fires.

Fast Cleaning: A large quantity of oil is used for deep frying. In addition to splattering while frying, there is leftover oil that can be difficult (and annoying) to dispose of after everything is cooked. There is no oil to get rid of since minimum oil is being used. The air fryer parts are a safe dishwasher making it easy to clean up.

Low-calorie food: Hot air fryers add little calories to food. Calories can be helpful at certain times, but too much is never a good option. This cooking tool avoids all of these unhealthy fats and keeps your food healthy at all times. Lowering calories can help you lose weight and help you lose weight if you have problems.

Little oil: The use of additional oils besides the food oil, which is fried, can be completely avoided. Hot air fryers work best when the food is dry and ungreased. This is much healthier than soaking food in oil using a traditional tempura pan.

Burning oil produces substances that are medically proven to cause cancer and cardiovascular problems such as heart failure. Furthermore, saving on oil purchases and saving money is not a bad thing.

Tips and Tricks of using Air Fryer

1. PRE-HEAT YOUR AIR FRYER... for a proper, it normal practice that any cooking item should be pre-heated. Often I do it, sometimes I don't do it, and my meal is still good. And in case your air fryer is without a pre-heat feature, simply turn it to the desired temperature and allow it to run for about 3 minutes before bringing adding the food.

2. USE OIL FOR FOODS COOKED IN THE AIR FRYER... I like using oils for certain foods to make them crisp, but some foods don't always need it.

3. DON'T OVERLOAD THE BASKET: If you want your fried food to turn out to be fresh, you'll want to make sure you don't congest the refrigerator. Placing too much food in the bowl will keep the food from stretching and browning. Cook your food in containers or invest in a larger air fryer to make sure this doesn't happen.

4. SHAKE THE BASKET DURING FRYING, WINGS, AND OTHER COOKING. When frying small items such as chicken wings and French fries, shake the basket every few minutes to ensure uniform cooking, sometimes, instead of throwing, use a pair of silicone kitchen pins to flip over larger items

5. SPRAY HALFWAY THROUGH COOKING: I find that spraying oil halfway through cooking is best done on most foods. Coated food items are to be sprayed. Additionally, spray some dried flour spots that still surface halfway through the rain.

6. WATER / BREAD IN THE BASE STOPS WHITE SMOKE: If it is time to fry a greasy food in your air fryer, don't be shocked to see some white smoke pouring out of the machine. To solve the problem, just dump a little (about 2Tbsp) of water in the bottom of the container, the smoke stops and the food continues to cook.

Some people place a slice of bread at the bottom of the unit to blot the grease when preparing items that can spread large amounts of grease, such as bacon.

7. LOOKOUT FOR THE SMALL LIGHT ITEMS IN THE AIR FRYER: most of the Air Fryer unit has a powerful fan at the top of the unit.

8. ADJUST THE TEMPERATURE: Most times, you want to turn the heat of the Air Fryer to the highest temperature to encourage it to work but be careful as some foods will dry out easily. A proper way is to adjust the temperature and time from how long you would usually do it in the oven. I like to go down 30 degrees and cut the time by about 20 percent. For starters, if you baked brownies at 350 degrees Fahrenheit in the oven for 20 minutes, cut the Air Fryer to 320 degrees and cook for about 16 minutes.

CHAPTER 3: OTHER TIPS USING THE AIR FRYER

Air fryers are designed to be super easy to use. Here's a little guide to get you started.

Choose a recipe

Choose a recipe that you can cook in your air fryer. Remember that most foods that you cook in your microwave or oven, or on the stovetop, can be prepared in the air fryer – except for those recipes that have a lot of fat or liquids. You can use my air fryer cookbook to help you find suitable recipes.

Prepare the air fryer

Read through the recipe to the end, so you know what accessories you need for cooking. Some recipes call for using the basket, rack, or rotisserie that comes with the air fryer. Other recipes use cake or muffin pans that you can insert into the air fryer. Just be sure these pans fit into the fryer and are safe to use.

Prepare the ingredients

Gather the ingredients for the recipe and prep them according to the instructions. When prepped, put the ingredients into the air fryer or in the basket, rack, or pans within the air fryer. Use parchment baking paper or a light mist of oil spray to prevent food from sticking.

Never crowd food in the air fryer or over-fill. Food that is crowded in the air fryer won't cook evenly and can be raw and under-cooked. If you're preparing for a crowd, you may have to cook more than one batch.

Setting the temperature and time

Check the recipe for the correct temperature and time setting. You can set it manually, r you can use the digital setting for the temperature and time needed for the recipe. Most air fryers also have preset functions that make it easy to set according to each recipe.

Check food during cooking

Many air fryer recipes require you to check the food while it's cooking so that it cooks evenly and doesn't over-cook. All you need to do is shake, flip, or toss the food to distribute it. Or for some recipes, you'll need to turn the food about halfway through when cooking so that it cooks and crisps thoroughly all the way through.

Cleaning the air fryer

Once the food is cooked, remove, and unplug the air fryer. Let it cool completely before cleaning. Follow the instructions that come with the fryer for proper cleaning. Never scrub or use abrasive cleaners when cleaning the fryer or the fryer accessories. What air fryer should you use?

The recipes in my book can be used with any model of an air fryer. This includes oven-style fryers that have horizontal racks or fryers that have a basket and handle.

My recipes were developed for my air fryer – it only has a temperature and timer setting. But you'll able to make any of the recipes in my book even if your air fryer has preset functions or multiple functions for baking, broiling, and roasting. Choose a function that matches my recipe or use the manual setting if you're unsure.

Using the basket or rack

Some models of air fryers use a round basket where foods are cooked while other models will have layered racks that fit into a square cooking space, much like a small oven. My recipes can be used for both baskets and racks.

Keep an eye on timing

You will find that air fryers cook at different temperatures depending on what model you have. This is why it's important to check on foods during the cooking process, so you don't over or undercook them. If you've cut back on quantities in some of my recipes, be sure to cut the cooking time down accordingly. Remember, my hints are just recommendations to guide you as you use your air fryer.

Using oil sprays

Most of my recipes in this book use oil spray – I use PAM. However, you can use any brand you want. Or make your own by merely putting olive oil into a small spray bottle. Use a small amount of oil and spray over the basket and trays to prevent food from sticking. Some of my recipes require you to spray the food with oil directly.

Function Keys

- **Button / Play/Pause Button**

This Play/Pause button allows you to pause during the middle of the cooking so you can shake the air fryer basket or flip the food to ensure it cooks evenly.

- **-/+ Button /Minus/Plus Button**

This button is used to change the time or temperature.

- **Keep Warm**

This function keeps your food warm for 30 minutes.

- **Food Presets**

This button gives you the ability to cook food without second-guessing. The time and temperature are already set, so new users find this setting useful.

- **Roast or Broil**

You can roast or broil with this setting. When using a conventional oven, you need to brown the meat before roasting. You can skip this step when cooking with an air fryer.

- **Dehydrate**

This setting cooks and dries food at a low temperature for a few hours. With this option, you can create your beef jerky or dried fruit.

CHAPTER 4: BREAKFAST

1. GRILLED PINEAPPLES WITH HONEY

A Perfect and Classic Recipe for Family Breakfast

Easy

20 minutes

Breakfast

2 Servings

INGREDIENTS

1 tsp cinnamon

5 pineapple slices

½ cup brown sugar

1 tbsp. basil, chopped for garnish

1 tbsp. honey, for garnish

COOKING STEPS

1. Preheat your Air fryer to 340 degrees F.

2. In a small bowl, mix brown sugar and cinnamon.

3. Drizzle the sugar mixture over your pineapple slices and set aside for 20 minutes.

4. Place the pineapple rings in the frying basket and cook for 10 minutes.

5. Flip the pineapples and cook for 10 minutes more.

6. Serve with basil and a drizzle of honey.

Nutrition: Calories 67.1, Fat 0.4g, Carbohydrates 17.1 g, Sugar 15 g, Protein 0.3 g.

2. PARMESAN SAUSAGE FRITTATA WITH TOMATOES

A Perfect and Classic Recipe for Family Breakfast

Easy

10 minutes

Breakfast

1 Servings

INGREDIENTS

½ sausage, chopped

Salt and black pepper to taste

A bunch of parsley, chopped

3 whole eggs

1 tbsp. olive oil

1 slice bread

4 cherry tomatoes, halved

1 slice bread

2 tbsp. parmesan, shredded for garnish

COOKING STEPS

1. Preheat your Air Fryer oven to 360 degrees F.

2. Place tomatoes and sausages in your air fryer's cooking basket and cook for 5 minutes.

3. In a bowl, mix baked tomatoes, sausages, eggs, salt, parsley, parmesan, oil, and pepper.

4. Add the bread to the frying basket and cook for 5 minutes.

5. Add the frittata mixture over baked bread and top with Parmesan cheese. Serve and enjoy!

Nutrition: Calories 152.7, Fat 10.1g, Carbohydrates 3.1 g, Sugar 0.8 g, Protein 12.8 g.

3. TOFU & GREEN ONION OMELET WITH SOY SAUCE

A Perfect and Classic Recipe for Family Breakfast

Easy

10 minutes

Breakfast

1 Servings

INGREDIENTS

1 small Japanese tofu, cubed

3 whole eggs

Pepper to taste

1 tsp coriander

1 tsp cumin

2 tbsp. soy sauce

2 tbsp. green onion, chopped

Olive oil

1 whole onion, chopped

COOKING STEPS

1. In a bowl, mix eggs, soy sauce, cumin, pepper, oil, and salt.

2. Add cubed tofu to baking forms and pour the egg mixture on top.

3. Place the prepared forms in the frying basket and cook for 10 minutes at 400 F.

4. Serve with a sprinkle of coriander and green onion.

Nutrition: Calories 195, Fat 15g, Carbohydrates 2 g, Sugar 1 g, Protein 12 g.

4. EGGS IN AVOCADO CUPS

A Perfect and Classic Recipe for Family Breakfast

Easy

22 minutes

Breakfast

2 Servings

INGREDIENTS

1 large ripe avocado, halved and pitted

2 eggs

Salt and ground black pepper, as required

2 tablespoons Parmesan cheese, grated

1 teaspoon fresh chives, minced

COOKING STEPS

1. With a spoon, scoop out some of the flesh from the avocado halves to make a whole.

2. Arrange the avocado halves onto a baking pan.

3. Crack one egg into each avocado half and sprinkle with salt and black pepper.

4. Arrange the "Wire Rack" at the middle position of the Air Fryer Toaster Oven and press "Preheat".

5. Select "Start/Cancel" to begin preheating.

6. When the unit beeps to show that it is preheated, arrange the baking pan on top of "Wire Rack".

7. Insert the "Wire Rack" at the middle position and select "Air Fry".

8. Set the temperature to 350 degrees F for 22 minutes.

9. Select "Start/Cancel" to begin cooking.

10. After 12 minutes of cooking, sprinkle the top of avocado halves with Parmesan cheese.

11. Select "Start/Cancel" to stop cooking.

12. Serve hot with the garnishing of chives.

Nutrition: Calories 286, Fat 25.2g, Carbohydrates 9 g, Sugar 0.9 g, Protein 9.5 g.

5. CLOUD EGGS

A Perfect and Classic Recipe for Family Breakfast

Easy

7 minutes

Breakfast

2 Servings

INGREDIENTS

2 eggs, whites, and yolks separated

Pinch of salt

Pinch of freshly ground black pepper

2 bread slices, toasted

COOKING STEPS

1. In a bowl, add the egg white, salt, and black pepper and beat until stiff peaks form.

2. Line a baking pan with parchment paper.

3. Carefully, make a pocket in the center of each egg white circle.

4. Arrange "Wire Rack" at the top position of the Air Fryer Toaster Oven and press "Preheat".

5. Select "Start/Cancel" to begin preheating.

6. When the unit beeps to show that it is preheated, arrange the baking pan on top of "Wire Rack".

7. Insert the "Wire Rack" at the top position and select "Broil.

8. Set the time for 7 minutes and Select "Start/Cancel" to begin cooking.

9. Place 1 egg yolk into each egg white pocket after 5 minutes of cooking.

10. Select "Start/Cancel" to stop cooking.

11. Serve alongside toasted bread slices.

Nutrition: Calories 87, Fat 4.7g, Carbohydrates 4.9 g, Sugar 0.7 g, Protein 6.2 g.

6. SAVORY PARSLEY SOUFFLÉ

A Perfect and Classic Recipe for Family Breakfast

Easy

8 minutes

Breakfast

2 Servings

INGREDIENTS

2 tablespoons light cream

2 eggs

1 tablespoon fresh parsley, chopped

1 fresh red chili pepper, chopped

Salt, as required

COOKING STEPS

1. Grease two soufflé dishes.

2. In a bowl, add all the ingredients and beat until well combined.

3. Divide the mixture into prepared soufflé dishes.

4. Arrange the "Inner Basket" in Air Fryer Toaster Oven and press "Preheat".

5. Select "Start/Cancel" to begin preheating.

6. When the unit beeps to show that it is preheated, arrange the soufflé dishes in the "Inner Basket".

7. Insert the "Inner Basket" and select "Air Fry".

8. Set the temperature to 390 degrees F for 8 minutes.

9. Select "Start/Cancel" to begin cooking.

10. Select "Start/Cancel" to stop cooking and serve hot.

Nutrition: Calories 108, Fat 9g, Carbohydrates 1.1 g, Sugar 0.5 g, Protein 6 g.

7. BACON, SPINACH & EGG CUPS

A Perfect and Classic Recipe for Family Breakfast

Easy

15 minutes

Breakfast

3 Servings

INGREDIENTS

3 eggs

6 cooked bacon slices, chopped

2 cups fresh baby spinach

1/3 cup heavy cream

3 tablespoons Parmesan cheese, grated

Salt and ground black pepper, as required

COOKING STEPS

1. Heat a nonstick skillet over medium-high heat and cook the bacon for about 5 minutes.

2. Add the spinach and cook for about 2-3 minutes.

3. Stir in the heavy cream and Parmesan cheese and cook for about 2-3 minutes.

4. Remove from the heat and set aside to cool slightly.

5. Grease three (3-inch) ramekins.

6. Crack one egg in each prepared ramekin and top with bacon mixture.

7. Arrange the "Inner Basket" in Air Fryer Toaster Oven and press "Preheat".

8. Select "Start/Cancel" to begin preheating.

9. When the unit beeps to show that it is preheated, arrange the ramekins in "Inner Basket".

10. Insert the "Inner Basket" and select "Air Fry".

11. Set the temperature to 350 degrees F for 4 minutes.

12. Select "Start/Cancel" to begin cooking.

13. Select "Start/Cancel" to stop cooking.

14. Sprinkle with salt and black pepper and serve hot.

Nutrition: Calories 442, Fat 34.7g, Carbohydrates 2.3 g, Sugar 0.4 g, Protein 29.6 g.

8. BLUEBERRY MUFFINS

A Perfect and Classic Recipe for Family Breakfast

Easy

15 minutes

Breakfast

3 Servings

INGREDIENTS

1 egg, beaten
1 ripe banana, peeled and mashed
1¼ cups almond flour
2 tablespoons granulated sugar
½ teaspoon baking powder
1 tablespoon coconut oil, melted
1/8 cup maple syrup
1 teaspoon apple cider vinegar
1 teaspoon vanilla extract
1 teaspoon lemon zest, grated
Pinch of ground cinnamon
½ cup fresh blueberries

COOKING STEPS

1. In a large bowl, add all the ingredients except blueberries and mix until well combined.

2. Gently, fold in the blueberries.

3. Grease a 6 cups muffin pan.

4. Place the mixture into prepared muffin cups about ¾ full.

5. Arrange the "Wire Rack" at the lower position of the Air Fryer Toaster Oven and press "Preheat".

6. Select "Start/Cancel" to begin preheating.

7. When the unit beeps to show that it is preheated, arrange the muffin pan on top of "Wire Rack".

8. Insert the "Wire Rack" at a lower position and select "Bake.

9. Set the temperature to 375 degrees F for 12 minutes.

10. Select "Start/Cancel" to begin cooking.

11. Select "Start/Cancel" to stop cooking.

12. Remove the muffin pan from the Air Fryer Toaster Oven and place onto a wire "Wire Rack" to cool for 10-15 minutes before serving.

Nutrition: Calories 23, Fat 14.7g, Carbohydrates 20.1 g, Sugar 12.5 g, Protein 6.2 g.

9. SAVORY SAUSAGE & BEANS MUFFINS

A Perfect and Classic Recipe for Family Breakfast

Easy

20 minutes

Breakfast

6 Servings

INGREDIENTS

4 eggs

½ cup cheddar cheese, shredded

3 tablespoons heavy cream

1 tablespoon tomato paste

¼ teaspoon salt

Pinch of freshly ground black pepper

Cooking spray

4 cooked breakfast sausage links, chopped

3 tablespoons baked beans

COOKING STEPS

1. Grease a 6 cups muffin pan.

2. In a bowl, add the eggs, cheddar cheese, heavy cream, tomato paste, salt, and black pepper, and beat until well combined.

3. Divide the mixture into prepared muffin cups evenly and top each with cooked sausage, followed by beans.

4. Arrange the "Wire Rack" at the middle position of the Air Fryer Toaster Oven and press "Preheat".

5. Select "Start/Cancel" to begin preheating.

6. When the unit beeps to show that it is preheated, arrange the muffin pan on top of "Wire Rack".

7. Insert the "Wire Rack" at the middle position and select "Bake.

8. Set the temperature to 350 degrees F for 20 minutes.

9. Select "Start/Cancel" to begin cooking.

10. Select "Start/Cancel" to stop cooking.

11. Remove the muffin pan from the Air Fryer Toaster Oven and place onto a wire "Wire Rack" to cool for 5 minutes before serving.

Nutrition: Calories 258, Fat 20.4g, Sugar 0.9 g, Protein 14.6 g.

10. MINI SPINACH QUICHES

A Perfect and Classic Recipe for Family Breakfast

Easy

25 minutes

Breakfast

6 Servings

INGREDIENTS

2 (9-inch) premade pie crusts, thawed

2 eggs

½ cup sharp cheddar cheese, shredded

¼ cup whole milk

¼ cup heavy cream

¼ cup frozen spinach, drained

Pinch of ground nutmeg

Pinch of garlic powder

Pinch of onion powder

Salt and ground black pepper, as required

COOKING STEPS

1. Cut the piecrust into six (3-inch) circles.

2. Lightly, grease a 6 cups muffin pan.

3. Arrange the circles into a 6 cups muffin pan.

4. With a fork, holes in the bottom of each pie crust and set aside.

5. In a bowl, add the remaining ingredients and beat until well combined.

6. Divide the mixture over each piecrust evenly.

7. Arrange the "Wire Rack" at the lower position of the Air Fryer Toaster Oven and select "Bake".

8. Press "Preheat" and set the temperature to 375 degrees F for 25 minutes.

9. Select "Start/Cancel" to begin preheating.

10. When the unit beeps to show that it is preheated, arrange the muffin pan on top of "Wire Rack".

11. Insert the "Wire Rack" at a lower position and select "Start/Cancel" to begin cooking.

12. Close the lid and select "Start/Cancel" to begin cooking.

Nutrition: Calories 329, Fat 22.9g, Carbohydrates 23.2 g, Sugar 0.8 g, Protein 7.7 g.

CHAPTER 5: SNACK AND APPETIZERS

11. COCONUT SHRIMPS

A Perfect Recipe for Snack and Appetizers

Easy

12 minutes

Snack and Appetizers

4 Servings

INGREDIENTS

8 ounces of coconut milk

½ cup panko breadcrumbs

8 large shrimp, peeled and deveined

Salt and ground black pepper, to taste

½ teaspoon cayenne pepper

COOKING STEPS

1. In a mixing bowl, add salt, black pepper, and coconut milk. Combine the ingredients to mix well with each other.

2. In another bowl, add breadcrumbs, cayenne pepper, Ground black pepper, and salt. Combine the ingredients to mix well with each other.

3. Coat shrimps with first coconut mixture and then with crumbs. Coat evenly.

4. Grease a baking pan with some cooking spray. Place shrimps over the pan.

5. Place Instant Vortex over the kitchen platform. Arrange to drip pan in the lower position. Press "Air Fry," set the timer to 15 minutes, and set the temperature to 350°F. Instant Vortex will start pre-heating.

6. When Instant Vortex is pre-heated, it will display "Add Food" on its screen. Open the door, and take out the middle roasting tray.

7. Place the pan over the tray and push it back; close the door and cooking will start. Midway, it will display "Turn Food" on its screen; flip shrimps, and close the door.

8. Open the door after the cooking cycle is over; serve warm.

Nutrition: Calories 209, Fat 15 g, Carbohydrates 6 g, Protein 4.5 g.

12. GUACAMOLE TORTILLA CHIPS

A Perfect Recipe for Snack and Appetizers

 Easy   15 minutes   **Snack and Appetizers**   4 Servings

INGREDIENTS

Chips:

1 tablespoon cumin powder

1 tablespoon paprika powder

12 corn tortillas

2 tablespoon olive oil

Ground black pepper and salt to taste

Guacamole:

1 small firm tomato, chopped

1 large avocado, pitted,

peeled, and mashed

A pinch dried parsley

COOKING STEPS

1. In a mixing bowl, add all chips ingredients. Combine the ingredients to mix well with each other.

2. In another bowl, add guacamole ingredients. Combine the ingredients to mix well with each other.

3. Place Instant Vortex over the kitchen platform. Arrange to drip pan in the lower position.

4. Press "Air Fry," set the timer to 15 minutes, and set the temperature to 375°F. Instant Vortex will start pre-heating.

5. In the rotisserie basket, add a chips mixture.

6. When Instant Vortex is pre-heated, it will display "Add Food" on its screen. Open the door and lock the basket. Press the red lever and arrange the basket on the left side; now, just simply rest the basket rod over the right side.

7. Close the door and press "Rotate"; cooking will start. Cook until chips are evenly golden.

8. Open the door after the cooking cycle is over; serve chips with guacamole.

Nutrition: Calories 140, Fat 13 g, Carbohydrates 11 g, Protein 2.5 g.

13. ROASTED CHICKPEAS

A Perfect Recipe for Snack and Appetizers

Easy

45 minutes

Snack and Appetizers

2 Servings

INGREDIENTS

1 (15 ounces) can chickpeas, drained
1/4 teaspoon garlic powder
1/4 teaspoon ground cumin
1/4 teaspoon ground coriander
1/4 teaspoon curry powder
1/8 teaspoon salt
1/4 teaspoon chili pepper powder
1/4 teaspoon paprika
Olive oil

COOKING STEPS

1. In a mixing bowl, add chickpeas and spices. Combine the ingredients to mix well with each other.

2. Place Instant Vortex over the kitchen platform. Arrange to drip pan in the lower position.

3. Press "Air Fry," set the timer to 35 minutes, and set the temperature to 375°F. Instant Vortex will start pre-heating.

4. In the rotisserie basket, add a chickpea mixture.

5. When Instant Vortex is pre-heated, it will display "Add Food" on its screen. Open the door and lock the basket. Press the red lever and arrange the basket on the left side; now, just simply rest the basket rod over the right side.

6. Close the door and press "Rotate"; cooking will start. Cook until evenly toasted and golden brown. Cook for 5-10 minutes more if needed.

7. Open the door after the cooking cycle is over; serve warm.

Nutrition: Calories 138, Fat 1.5 g, Carbohydrates 15 g, Protein 4 g.

14. SUPREME FRENCH FRIES

A Perfect Recipe for Snack and Appetizers

Easy

30 minutes

Snack and Appetizers

4 Servings

INGREDIENTS

½ teaspoon onion powder

½ teaspoon garlic powder

1 pound potatoes, peeled and cut into strips

3 tablespoons olive oil

1 teaspoon paprika

Salt to taste (optional)

COOKING STEPS

1. In a mixing bowl, add potato strips and water. Soak for an hour; drain and dry pieces completely over paper towels.

2. In a mixing bowl, add a strip and other ingredients. Combine the ingredients to mix well with each other.

3. Place Instant Vortex over the kitchen platform. Arrange to drip pan in the lower position.

4. Press "Air Fry," set the timer to 30 minutes, and set the temperature to 375°F. Instant Vortex will start pre-heating.

5. In the rotisserie basket, add potato mix.

6. When Instant Vortex is pre-heated, it will display "Add Food" on its screen. Open the door and lock the basket. Press the red lever and arrange the basket on the left side; now, just simply rest the basket rod over the right side.

7. Close the door and press "Rotate"; cooking will start.

8. Open the door after the cooking cycle is over; serve warm.

Nutrition: Calories 176, Fat 11 g, Carbohydrates 17 g, Protein 3 g.

15. BUTTER CASHEWS

A Perfect Recipe for Snack and Appetizers

Easy

5 minutes

Snack and Appetizers

5/6 Servings

INGREDIENTS

1 teaspoon butter, melted

1 ½ cups raw cashew nuts

Salt and black pepper to taste

COOKING STEPS

1. In a mixing bowl, add cashews and other ingredients. Combine the ingredients to mix well with each other.

2. Grease a baking tray with some cooking spray. Place cashews over the tray.

3. Place Instant Vortex over the kitchen platform. Arrange to drip pan in the lower position.

4. Press "Air Fry," set the timer to 5 minutes, and set the temperature to 355°F. Instant Vortex will start pre-heating.

5. When Instant Vortex is pre-heated, it will display "Add Food" on its screen. Open the door, and take out the middle roasting tray.

6. Place the baking tray over the roasting tray and push it back; close the door and cooking will start. Midway it will display "Turn Food" on its screen; shake the baking tray and close the door.

7. Open the door after the cooking cycle is over; serve warm.

Nutrition: Calories 233, Fat 15 g, Carbohydrates 12 g, Protein 6 g.

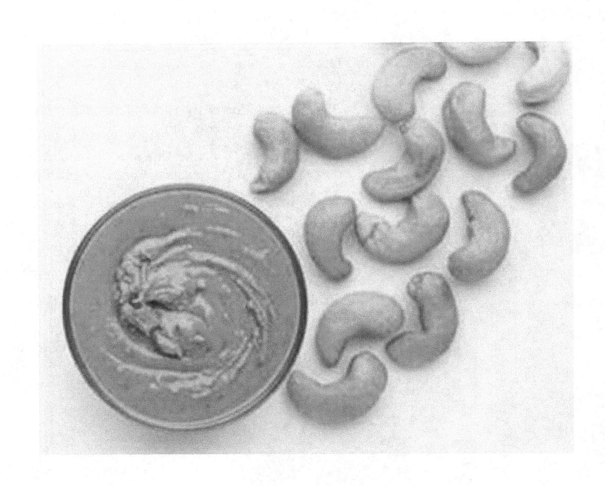

16. CINNAMON BANANA CHIPS

A Perfect Recipe for Snack and Appetizers

Easy

6 minutes

Snack and Appetizers

4 Servings

INGREDIENTS

¼ teaspoon of cocoa powder

A pinch of cinnamon powder

5 large firm banana, peeled

COOKING STEPS

1. Slice bananas thinly in a horizontal manner and combine with cocoa and cinnamon in a bowl.

2. Place Instant Vortex over the kitchen platform. Arrange to drip pan in the lower position.

3. Press "Air Fry," set the timer to 7 minutes, and set the temperature to 380°F. Instant Vortex will start pre-heating.

4. When Instant Vortex is pre-heated, it will display "Add Food" on its screen. Open the door, and take out the middle roasting tray.

5. Place slices (cook in batches if needed) over the tray and push it back; close the door and cooking will start. Midway, it will display "Turn Food" on its screen; ignore it, and it will continue to cook after 10 seconds. Cook until the slices crisps.

6. Open the door after the cooking cycle is over; serve warm.

Nutrition: Calories 233, Fat 15 g, Carbohydrates 12 g, Protein 6 g.

17. BASIL TOMATOES

A Perfect Recipe for Vegetable

 Easy

 10 minutes

 vegetable recipes

 2 Servings

INGREDIENTS

3 tomatoes, halved

Olive oil cooking spray

Salt and ground black pepper, as required

1 tablespoon fresh basil, chopped

COOKING STEPS

1. Drizzle cut sides of the tomato halves with cooking spray evenly.

2. Sprinkle with salt, black pepper, and basil.

3. Press the "Power Button" of the Air Fry Oven and turn the dial to select the "Air Fry" mode.

4. Press the Time button and again turn the dial to set the cooking time to 10 minutes.

5. Now push the Temp button and rotate the dial to set the temperature at 320 degrees F.

6. Press the "Start/Pause" button to start.

7. When the unit beeps to show that it is preheated, open the lid.

8. Arrange the tomatoes in "Air Fry Basket" and insert them in the oven.

9. Serve warm.

Nutrition: Calories 34, Fat 0.4 g, Carbohydrates 7.2 g, Sugar 4.9, Protein 1.7 g.

18. PESTO TOMATOES
A Perfect Recipe for Vegetable

Easy

14 minutes

vegetable recipes

4 Servings

INGREDIENTS

3 large heirloom tomatoes cut into ½-inch thick slices.

1 cup pesto

8 oz. feta cheese, cut into ½-inch thick slices.

½ cup red onions, sliced thinly

1 tablespoon olive oil

COOKING STEPS

1. Spread some pesto on each slice of tomato.

2. Top each tomato slice with a feta slice and onion and drizzle with oil.

3. Press the "Power Button" of the Air Fry Oven and turn the dial to select the "Air Fry" mode.

4. Press the Time button and again turn the dial to set the cooking time to 14 minutes.

5. Now push the Temp button and rotate the dial to set the temperature at 390 degrees F.

6. Press the "Start/Pause" button to start.

7. When the unit beeps to show that it is preheated, open the lid.

8. Arrange the tomatoes in a greased "Air Fry Basket" and insert them in the oven.

9. Serve warm.

Nutrition: Calories 480, Fat 41.9 g, Carbohydrates 13 g, Sugar 10.5, Protein 15.4 g.

19. STUFFED TOMATOES

A Perfect Recipe for Vegetable

Easy

15 minutes

vegetable recipes

2 Servings

INGREDIENTS

2 large tomatoes

½ cup broccoli, chopped finely

½ cup Cheddar cheese, shredded

Salt and ground black pepper, as required

1 tablespoon unsalted butter, melted

½ teaspoon dried thyme, crushed

COOKING STEPS

1. Carefully, cut the top of each tomato and scoop out pulp and seeds.

2. In a bowl, mix chopped broccoli, cheese, salt, and black pepper.

3. Stuff each tomato with broccoli mixture evenly.

4. Press the "Power Button" of the Air Fry Oven and turn the dial to select the "Air Fry" mode.

5. Press the Time button and again turn the dial to set the cooking time to 15 minutes.

6. Now push the Temp button and rotate the dial to set the temperature at 355 degrees F.

7. Press the "Start/Pause" button to start.

8. When the unit beeps to show that it is preheated, open the lid.

9. Arrange the tomatoes in a greased "Air Fry Basket" and insert them in the oven.

10. Serve warm with the garnishing of thyme.

Nutrition: Calories 206, Fat 15.6 g, Carbohydrates 9 g.

20. PARMESAN ASPARAGUS

A Perfect Recipe for Vegetable

Easy

10 minutes

vegetable recipes

3 Servings

INGREDIENTS

1 lb. fresh asparagus, trimmed

1 tablespoon Parmesan cheese, grated

1 tablespoon butter, melted

1 teaspoon garlic powder

Salt and ground black pepper, as required

COOKING STEPS

1. In a bowl, mix the asparagus, cheese, butter, garlic powder, salt, and black pepper.

2. Press the "Power Button" of the Air Fry Oven and turn the dial to select the "Air Fry" mode.

3. Press the Time button and again turn the dial to set the cooking time to 10 minutes.

4. Now push the Temp button and rotate the dial to set the temperature at 400 degrees F.

5. Press the "Start/Pause" button to start.

6. When the unit beeps to show that it is preheated, open the lid.

7. Arrange the veggie mixture in a greased "Air Fry Basket" and insert it in the oven.

8. Serve hot.

Nutrition: Calories 73, Fat 4.4 g, Carbohydrates 6.6 g, Sugar 3.1 g, Protein 4.2 g

21. ALMOND ASPARAGUS

A Perfect Recipe for Vegetable

Easy

6 minutes

vegetable recipes

3 Servings

INGREDIENTS

1 lb. asparagus

2 tablespoons olive oil

2 tablespoons balsamic vinegar

Salt and ground black pepper, as required

1/3 cup almonds, sliced

COOKING STEPS

1. In a bowl, mix the asparagus, oil, vinegar, salt, and black pepper.

2. Press the "Power Button" of the Air Fry Oven and turn the dial to select the "Air Fry" mode.

3. Press the Time button and again turn the dial to set the cooking time to 6minutes.

4. Now push the Temp button and rotate the dial to set the temperature at 400 degrees F.

5. Press the "Start/Pause" button to start.

6. When the unit beeps to show that it is preheated, open the lid.

7. Arrange the veggie mixture in a greased "Air Fry Basket" and insert it in the oven.

8. Serve hot.

Nutrition: Calories 173, Fat 14.4 g, Carbohydrates 8.2 g, Sugar 3.3 g, Protein 5.6 g

22. SPICY BUTTERNUT SQUASH

A Perfect Recipe for Vegetable

 Easy

 20 minutes

 vegetable recipes

 4 Servings

INGREDIENTS

1 medium butternut squash, peeled, seeded, and cut into chunk

2 teaspoons cumin seeds

1/8 teaspoon garlic powder

1/8 teaspoon chili flakes, crushed

Salt and ground black pepper, as required

1 tablespoon olive oil

2 tablespoons pine nuts

2 tablespoons fresh cilantro, chopped

COOKING STEPS

1. In a bowl, mix the squash, spices, and oil.

2. Press the "Power Button" of the Air Fry Oven and turn the dial to select the "Air Fry" mode.

3. Press the Time button and again turn the dial to set the cooking time to 20 minutes.

4. Now push the Temp button and rotate the dial to set the temperature at 375 degrees F.

5. Press the "Start/Pause" button to start.

6. When the unit beeps to show that it is preheated, open the lid.

7. Arrange the squash chunks in a greased "Air Fry Basket" and insert it in the oven.

8. Serve hot with the garnishing of pine nuts and cilantro.

Nutrition: Calories 191, Fat 7 g, Carbohydrates 34.3 g, Sugar 6.4 g, Protein 3.7 g

23. SWEET & SPICY PARSNIPS

A Perfect Recipe for Vegetable

Easy

44 minutes

vegetable recipes

5 Servings

INGREDIENTS

1½ lbs. parsnip, peeled and cut into 1-inch chunks

1 tablespoon butter, melted

2 tablespoons honey

1 tablespoon dried parsley flakes, crushed

¼ teaspoon red pepper flakes, crushed

Salt and ground black pepper, as required

COOKING STEPS

1. In a large bowl, mix the parsnips and butter.

2. Press the "Power Button" of the Air Fry Oven and turn the dial to select the "Air Fry" mode.

3. Press the Time button and again turn the dial to set the cooking time to 44 minutes.

4. Now push the Temp button and rotate the dial to set the temperature at 355 degrees F.

5. Press the "Start/Pause" button to start.

6. When the unit beeps to show that it is preheated, open the lid.

7. Arrange the squash chunks in a greased "Air Fry Basket" and insert it in the oven.

8. Meanwhile, in another large bowl, mix the remaining ingredients.

9. After 40 minutes of cooking, press the "Start/Pause" button to pause the unit.

10. Transfer the parsnips chunks into the bowl of honey mixture and toss to coat well.

11. Again, arrange the parsnip chunks in "Air Fry Basket" and insert it in the oven.

12. Serve hot.

Nutrition: Calories 191, Fat 7 g, Carbohydrates 34.3 g, Sugar 6.4 g, Protein 3.7 g

24. CAJUN PORK STEAKS

A Perfect Classic Recipe for Pork

Easy

20 minutes

Pork Recipes

6 Servings

INGREDIENTS

4-6 pork steaks
BBQ sauce:
Cajun seasoning
1 tbsp. vinegar
1 tsp. low-sodium soy sauce
½ C. brown sugar
½ C. vegan ketchup

COOKING STEPS

1. Ensure your Cuisinart Air Fryer Oven is preheated to 290 degrees.

2. Sprinkle pork steaks with Cajun seasoning.

3. Combine remaining ingredients and brush onto steaks. Add coated steaks to the air fryer.

4. Pour into the Oven rack/basket. Place the Rack on the middle-shelf of the Cuisinart Air Fryer Oven. Set temperature to 290°F, and set time to 20 minutes. Cook 15-20 minutes till just browned.

Nutrition: Calories 209, Fat 11 g, Sugar 2 g, Protein 28 g.

25. CAJUN SWEET-SOUR GRILLED PORK

A Perfect Classic Recipe for Pork

Easy

12 minutes

Pork Recipes

3 Servings

INGREDIENTS

¼ cup brown sugar

1/4 cup cider vinegar

1-lb pork loin, sliced into 1-inch cubes

2 tablespoons Cajun seasoning

3 tablespoons brown sugar

COOKING STEPS

1. In a shallow dish, mix well pork loin, 3 tablespoons brown sugar, and Cajun seasoning. Toss well to coat. Marinate in the ref for 3 hours.

2. In a medium bowl, mix well, brown sugar, and vinegar for basting.

3. Thread pork pieces in skewers. Baste with sauce and place on a skewer rack in the air fryer.

4. For 12 minutes, cook at 360°F. Halfway through cooking time, turnover skewers, and baste with sauce. If needed, cook in batches.

5. Serve and enjoy.

Nutrition: Calories 428, Fat 16.7 g, Sugar 2 g, Protein 39 g.

26. CHINESE BRAISED PORK BELLY

A Perfect Classic Recipe for Pork

Easy

20 minutes

Pork Recipes

8 Servings

INGREDIENTS

1 lb. Pork Belly, sliced

1 Tbsp. Oyster Sauce

1 Tbsp. Sugar

2 Red Fermented Bean Curds

1 Tbsp. Red Fermented Bean Curd Paste

1 Tbsp. Cooking Wine

1/2 Tbsp. Soy Sauce

1 Tsp Sesame Oil

1 cup All-Purpose Flour

COOKING STEPS

1. Preheat the Cuisinart Air Fryer Oven to 390 degrees.

2. In a small bowl, mix all ingredients and rub the pork thoroughly with this mixture

3. Set aside to marinate for at least 30 minutes or preferably overnight for the flavors to permeate the meat

4. Coat each marinated pork belly slice in flour and place in the air fryer tray

5. Cook for 15 to 20 minutes until crispy and tender.

Nutrition: Calories 1546, Fat 23 g, Carbohydrates 2 g, Protein 7 g.

27. AIR FRYER SWEET AND SOUR PORK

A Perfect Classic Recipe for Pork

Easy

12 minutes

Pork Recipes

6 Servings

INGREDIENTS

3 tbsp. olive oil

1/16 tsp. Chinese Five Spice

¼ tsp. pepper

½ tsp. sea salt

1 tsp. pure sesame oil

2 eggs

1 C. almond flour

2 pounds pork, sliced into chunks

Sweet and Sour Sauce:

¼ tsp. sea salt

½ tsp. garlic powder

1 tbsp. low-sodium soy sauce

½ C. rice vinegar

5 tbsp. tomato paste

1/8 tsp. water

½ C. sweetener of choice

COOKING STEPS

1. To make the dipping sauce, whisk all sauce ingredients together over medium heat, stirring for 5 minutes. Simmer uncovered for 5 minutes until thickened.

2. Meanwhile, combine almond flour, five-spice, pepper, and salt.

3. In another bowl, mix eggs with sesame oil.

4. Dredge pork in flour mixture and then in the egg mixture. Shake any excess off before adding to the air fryer basket.

5. Pour into the Oven rack/basket. Place the Rack on the middle-shelf of the Cuisinart Air Fryer Oven. Set temperature to 340°F, and set time to 12 minutes. Serve with sweet and sour dipping sauce.

Nutrition: Calories 371, Fat 17 g, Sugar 1 g, Protein 27 g.

28. PORK LOIN WITH POTATOES

A Perfect Classic Recipe for Pork

 Easy

 25 minutes

 Pork Recipes

 2 Servings

INGREDIENTS

2 pounds pork loin

1 teaspoon fresh parsley, chopped

2 large red potatoes, chopped

½ teaspoon garlic powder

½ teaspoon red pepper flakes, crushed

Salt and freshly ground black pepper, to taste

COOKING STEPS

1. In a large bowl, add all ingredients except glaze and toss to coat well. Preheat the Cuisinart Air Fryer Oven to 325 degrees F. Place the loin in the air fryer basket.

2. Arrange the potatoes around the pork loin.

3. Cook for about 25 minutes.

Nutrition: Calories 366, Fat 17 g, Sugar 14 g, Protein 28 g.

29. FRIED PORK SCOTCH EGG

A Perfect Classic Recipe for Pork

Easy

25 minutes

Pork Recipes

2 Servings

INGREDIENTS

3 soft-boiled eggs, peeled

8 ounces of raw minced pork, or sausage outside the casings

2 teaspoons of ground rosemary

2 teaspoons of garlic powder

Pinch of salt and pepper

2 raw eggs

1 cup of breadcrumbs (Panko, but other brands are fine, or home-made bread crumbs work too)

COOKING STEPS

1. Cover the basket of the air fryer with a lining of tin foil, leaving the edges uncovered to allow air to circulate through the basket. Preheat the Cuisinart Air Fryer Oven to 350 degrees.

2. In a mixing bowl, combine the raw pork with rosemary, garlic powder, salt, and pepper. This will probably be easiest to do with your masher or bare hands (though make sure to wash thoroughly after handling raw meat!); combine until all the spices are evenly spread throughout the meat.

3. Divide the meat mixture into three equal portions in the mixing bowl, and form each into balls with your hands.

4. Lay a large sheet of plastic wrap on the countertop, and flatten one of the balls of meat on top of it, to form a wide, flat meat-circle.

5. Place one of the peeled soft-boiled eggs in the center of the meat-circle and then, using the ends of the plastic wrap, pull the meat-circle so that it is fully covering and surrounding the soft-boiled egg.

6. Tighten and shape the plastic wrap covering the meat so that it forms a ball, and make sure not to squeeze too hard lest you squish the soft-boiled egg at the center of the ball! Set aside.

7. Repeat steps 5-7 with the other two soft-boiled eggs and portions of the meat mixture.

8. In a separate mixing bowl, beat the two raw eggs until fluffy and until the yolks and whites are fully combined.

9. One by one, remove the plastic wrap and dunk the pork-covered balls into the raw egg, and then roll them in the bread crumbs, covering fully and generously.

10. Place each of the bread-crumb covered meat-wrapped balls onto the foil-lined surface of the air fryer. Three of them should fit nicely, without touching.

11. Set the Cuisinart Air Fryer Oven timer to 25 minutes.

12. About halfway through the cooking time, shake the handle of the air-fryer vigorously, so that the scotch eggs inside roll around and ensure full coverage.

13. After 25 minutes, the air fryer will shut off and the scotch eggs should be perfect – the meat fully cooked, the egg-yolks still runny on the inside, and the outsides crispy and golden-brown. Using tongs, place them on serving plates, slice in half, and enjoy

Nutrition: Calories 481, Fat 34 g, Carbohydrates 18 g, Protein 20 g.

30. GARLIC ROSEMARY PORK CHOPS

A Perfect Classic Recipe for Pork

Easy

25 minutes

Pork Recipes

4 Servings

INGREDIENTS

4 pork chops, boneless and cut 1/2-inch thick

tsp dried rosemary, crushed

garlic cloves, minced

1/4 tsp pepper

1/4 tsp salt

COOKING STEPS

1. Insert wire rack in rack position 6. Select bake, set temperature 350 F, timer for 35 minutes. Press start to preheat the oven.

2. Season pork chops with pepper and salt.

3. In a small bowl, mix garlic and rosemary and rub all over pork chops.

4. Place pork chops on roasting pan and roast for 35 minutes.

5. Serve and enjoy.

Nutrition: Calories 208, Fat 16 g, Carbohydrates 0.6 g, Protein 14 g.

31. ROTISSERIE HONEY PORK

A Perfect Classic Recipe for Pork

Easy

20 minutes

Pork Recipes

2-3 Servings

INGREDIENTS

2 teaspoon sriracha hot sauce

½ teaspoon kosher salt

teaspoon honey

1-pound pork tenderloin

COOKING STEPS

1. Through pork tenderloin pierce rotisserie rod; secure it on both sides using forks.

2. In a mixing bowl, add salt, sriracha, and honey. Combine the ingredients to mix well with each other.

3. Brush tenderloin with honey mixture.

4. Place Instant Vortex over the kitchen platform. Arrange to drip pan in the lower position. Press "Roast," (You can also use Air Fry Setting) set the timer to 20 minutes and set the temperature to 375°F. Instant Vortex will start pre-heating.

5. When Instant Vortex is pre-heated, it will display "Add Food" on its screen. Open the door and lock the basket. Press the red lever and arrange the road on the left side; now, just simply rest the rod over the right side.

6. Close the door and press "Rotate"; cooking will start.

7. Open the door after the cooking cycle is over; slice and serve warm.

Nutrition: Calories 131, Fat 3 g, Carbohydrates 5.5 g, Protein 21 g.

32. PORK OLIVE SALAD
A Perfect Classic Recipe for Pork

Easy

20 minutes

Pork Recipes

4 Servings

INGREDIENTS

2 tablespoons olive oil
garlic clove, crushed
1 ¼ pound boneless pork, diced
teaspoons balsamic vinegar
Salad:
1 handful black olives, chopped
9-ounce feta cheese, crumbled
large tomatoes, chopped
1 cucumber, chopped
1 bunch of parsley, chopped

COOKING STEPS

1. In a mixing bowl, add balsamic vinegar, garlic, and olive oil. Combine the ingredients to mix well with each other.

2. Add and toss in pork cube. Marinate for 30 minutes in the refrigerator.

3. Take skewers and thread pork cubes. Grease a baking pan with some cooking spray. Place skewers over the pan.

4. Place Instant Vortex over the kitchen platform. Arrange to drip pan in the lower position. Press "Air Fry," set the timer to 20 minutes, and set the temperature to 360°F. Instant Vortex will start pre-heating.

5. When Instant Vortex is pre-heated, it will display "Add Food" on its screen. Open the door, and take out the middle roasting tray.

6. Place the pan over the tray and push it back; close the door and cooking will start. Midway, it will display "Turn Food" on its screen; flip skewers, and close the door.

7. Open the door after the cooking cycle is over.

8. In a mixing bowl, add salad ingredients. Combine the ingredients to mix well with each other. Serve pork cubes with salad on the side.

Nutrition: Calories 396, Fat 19 g, Carbohydrates 30 g, Protein 23 g.

33. HERB PORK ROAST
A Perfect Classic Recipe for Pork

 Easy   1 hour 30 minutes   **Pork Recipes**   6 Servings

INGREDIENTS

3 lbs. pork roast, boneless
2 fresh oregano sprigs
1/4 tbsp. black pepper
2 fresh thyme sprigs
cup of water
1 onion, chopped
garlic cloves, chopped
1 rosemary sprig
1 tbsp. olive oil
1 tbsp. kosher salt

COOKING STEPS

1. Insert wire rack in rack position 6. Select roast, set temperature 350 F, timer for 1 hour 30 minutes. Press start to preheat the oven.

2. Season pork roast with pepper and salt.

3. Heat olive oil in a stockpot and sear pork roast on each side, about 4 minutes.

4. Add onion and garlic. Pour in the water, oregano, and thyme and bring to boil for a minute.

5. Cover pot and roast in the preheated oven for 1 hour 30 minutes.

6. Serve and enjoy.

Nutrition: Calories 502, Fat 23.8 g, Carbohydrates 2.9 g, Protein 65.1 g.

34. CHARRED ONIONS AND STEAK CUBE BBQ

A Perfect Classic Recipe for Beef

Easy

40 minutes

Beef Recipes

3 Servings

INGREDIENTS

cup red onions, cut into wedges

1 tablespoon dry mustard

1 tablespoon olive oil

1-pound boneless beef sirloin, cut into cubes

Salt and pepper to taste

COOKING STEPS

1. Preheat the air fryer to 390°F.

2. Place the grill pan accessory in the air fryer.

3. Toss all ingredients in a bowl and mix until everything is coated with the seasonings.

4. Place on the grill pan and cook for 40 minutes.

5. Halfway through the cooking time, give a stir to cook evenly.

Nutrition: Calories 260, Fat 10 g, Protein 35 g.

35. BEEF STROGANOFF

A Perfect Classic Recipe for Beef

Easy

14 minutes

Beef Recipes

4 Servings

INGREDIENTS

9 Oz's Tender Beef

Onion, chopped

1 Tbsp. Paprika

3/4 Cup Sour Cream

Salt and Pepper to taste

Baking Dish

COOKING STEPS

1. Preheat the Cosori Air Fryer Oven to 390 degrees.

2. Chop the beef and marinate it using paprika.

3. Add the chopped onions into the baking dish and heat for about 2 minutes in the Cosori Air Fryer Oven.

4. Add the beef into the dish when the onions are transparent, and cook for 5 minutes.

5. Once the beef is starting to tender, pour in the sour cream and cook for another seven minutes.

6. At this point, the liquid should have reduced. Season with salt and pepper and serve.

Nutrition: Calories 391, Fat 23 g, Carbohydrates 21 g, Protein 25 g.

36. CHEESY GROUND BEEF AND MAC TACO CASSEROLE

A Perfect Classic Recipe for Beef

Easy

25 minutes

Beef Recipes

5 Servings

INGREDIENTS

1-ounce shredded Cheddar cheese

1-ounce shredded Monterey Jack cheese

2 tablespoons chopped green onions

1/2 (10.75 ounces) can condensed tomato soup

1/2-pound lean ground beef

1/2 cup crushed tortilla chips

1/4-pound macaroni, cooked according to manufacturer's Instructions

1/4 cup chopped onion

1/4 cup sour cream (optional)

1/2 (1.25 ounce) package taco seasoning mix

1/2 (14.5 ounces) can diced tomatoes

COOKING STEPS

1. Lightly grease the baking pan of the air fryer with cooking spray. Add onion and ground beef. For 10 minutes, cook at 360°F. Halfway through cooking time, stir and crumble ground beef.

2. Add taco seasoning, diced tomatoes, and tomato soup. Mix well. Mix in pasta.

3. Sprinkle crushed tortilla chips. Sprinkle cheese.

4. Cook for 15 minutes at 390°F until tops are lightly browned and cheese is melted.

5. Serve and enjoy.

Nutrition: Calories 329, Fat 17 g, Protein 15 g.

37. BEEFY STEAK TOPPED WITH CHIMICHURRI SAUCE

A Perfect Classic Recipe for Beef

Easy

25 minutes

Beef Recipes

5 Servings

INGREDIENTS

cup commercial chimichurri
pounds steak
Salt and pepper to taste

COOKING STEPS

1. Place all ingredients in a Ziploc bag and marinate in the fridge for 2 hours.

2. Preheat the air fryer to 390°F.

3. Place the grill pan accessory in the air fryer.

4. Grill the skirt steak for 20 minutes per batch.

5. Flip the steak every 10 minutes for even grilling.

Nutrition: Calories 507, Fat 27 g, Protein 63 g.

38. BEEF RIBEYE STEAK

A Perfect Classic Recipe for Beef

Easy

20 minutes

Beef Recipes

4 Servings

INGREDIENTS

4 (8-ounce) ribeye steaks
tablespoon McCormick Grill Mates Montreal Steak Seasoning
Salt
Pepper

COOKING STEPS

1. Season the steaks with the steak seasoning and salt and pepper to taste. Place 2 steaks in the Cosori Air Fryer Oven. You can use an accessory grill pan, a layer rack, or the air fryer basket.

2. Cook for 4 minutes. Open the air fryer and flip the steaks.

3. Cook for an additional four to five minutes. Check for doneness to determine how much additional Cooking Time: is a need. Remove the cooked steaks from the Cosori Air Fryer Oven, and then repeat for the remaining two steaks. Cool before serving.

Nutrition: Calories 29, Fat 22 g, Protein 23 g.

39. BEEF KORMA

A Perfect Classic Recipe for Beef

Easy

20 minutes

Beef Recipes

6 Servings

INGREDIENTS

½ cup yogurt

tablespoon curry powder

1 tablespoon olive oil

1 onion, chopped

cloves garlic, minced

1 tomato, diced

½ cup frozen baby peas, thawed

COOKING STEPS

1. In a medium bowl, combine the steak, yogurt, and curry powder. Stir and set aside.

2. In a 6-inch metal bowl, combine the olive oil, onion, and garlic.

3. Cook for 3 to 4 minutes or until crisp and tender.

4. Add the steak along with the yogurt and the diced tomato. Cook for 12 to 13 minutes or until the steak is almost tender.

5. Stir in the peas and cook for 2 to 3 minutes or until hot.

Nutrition: Calories 289, Fat 11 g, Fiber 2 g, Protein 38 g.

40. CUMIN-PAPRIKA RUBBED BEEF BRISKET

A Perfect Classic Recipe for Beef

Easy

2 hours

Beef Recipes

12 Servings

INGREDIENTS

¼ teaspoon cayenne pepper

½ tablespoons paprika

1 teaspoon garlic powder

1 teaspoon ground cumin

1 teaspoon onion powder

teaspoons dry mustard

teaspoons ground black pepper

2 teaspoons salt

pounds brisket roast

tablespoons olive oil

COOKING STEPS

1. Place all ingredients in a Ziploc bag and allow marinating in the fridge for at least 2 hours.

2. Preheat the Cosori Air Fryer Oven for 5 minutes.

3. Place the meat in a baking dish that will fit in the air fryer.

4. Place in the air fryer and cook for 2 hours at 350°F.

Nutrition: Calories 269, Fat 12 g, Fiber 2 g, Protein 35 g.

41. RANCH FLAVORED TILAPIA

A Perfect Classic Recipe for Fish

| Easy | 13 minutes | **Fish Recipes** | 4 Servings |

INGREDIENTS

¾ cup cornflakes, crushed

1-ounce dry ranch mix

2 and ½ tablespoons vegetable oil

2 whole eggs

4 pieces 6 ounces each tilapia fillets

COOKING STEPS

1. Take a shallow bowl, crack in eggs, and beat them well

2. Take another bowl and add cornflakes, ranch dressing, oil, and mix well until you have a crumbly ix

3. Dip fish fillets into the egg, coat well with bread crumbs mixture

4. Press "Power Button" on your Air Fryer and select "Air Fry" mode

5. Press the Time Button and set the time to 13 minutes

6. Push Temp Button and set temp to 356 degrees F

7. Press the "Start/Pause" button and start the device

8. Once the appliance beeps to indicated that it is pre-heated, arrange prepared tilapia into Air Fryer basket, insert it into the oven

9. Let it cook until done, serve, and enjoy!

Nutrition: Calories 267, Fat 12 g, Carbohydrates 5 g, Protein 34 g.

42. BUTTER UP SALMON
A Perfect Classic Recipe for Fish

Easy

10 minutes

Fish Recipes

2 Servings

INGREDIENTS

2 pieces 6 ounces salmon fillets
Salt and pepper to taste
tablespoon butter, melted

COOKING STEPS

1. Season salmon fillet well with salt and pepper, coat them with butter

2. Press "Power Button" on your Air Fryer and select "Air Fry" mode

3. Press the Time Button and set the time to 20 minutes

4. Push Temp Button and set temp to 320 degrees F

5. Press the "Start/Pause" button and start the device

6. Once the appliance beeps to indicated that it is pre-heated, transfer fillets to a greased Air Fryer basket and push them into the oven

7. Serve and enjoy!

Nutrition: Calories 270, Fat 16 g, Carbohydrates 0 g, Protein 33 g.

43. LEMON SALMON

A Perfect Classic Recipe for Fish

Easy

8 minutes

Fish Recipes

3 Servings

INGREDIENTS

½ pounds salmon

½ teaspoon red chili powder

Salt and pepper to taste

1 lemon, cut into slices

1 tablespoon fresh dill, chopped

COOKING STEPS

1. Season salmon with chili powder, salt, pepper generously

2. Press "Power Button" on your Air Fryer and select "Air Fry" mode

3. Press the Time Button and set time to 8 minutes

4. Push Temp Button and set temp to 375 degrees F

5. Press the "Start/Pause" button and start the device

6. Once the appliance beeps to indicated that it is pre-heated, arrange salmon fillets in the Air Fryer cooking basket

7. Push into Air Fryer Oven and cook until the timer runs out

8. Garnish with fresh dill and serve hot!

Nutrition: Calories 305, Fat 14 g, Carbohydrates 1.3 g, Protein 44 g.

44. HEARTY SPICED SALMON

A Perfect Classic Recipe for Fish

Easy

11 minutes

Fish Recipes

2 Servings

INGREDIENTS

teaspoon smoked paprika

1 teaspoon cayenne pepper

1 teaspoon onion powder

1 teaspoon garlic powder

Salt and pepper to taste

pieces 6 ounces salmon fillets

teaspoons olive oil

COOKING STEPS

1. Take a small bowl and add spices, mix them well

2. Drizzle salmon fillets with oil, rub the fillets with spice mixture

3. Press "Power Button" on your Air Fryer and select "Air Fry" mode

4. Press the Time Button and set the time to 11 minutes

5. Push Temp Button and set temp to 390 degrees F

6. Press the "Start/Pause" button and start the device

7. Once the appliance beeps to indicated that it is pre-heated, arrange salmon fillets in the Air Fryer cooking basket

8. Push into Air Fryer Oven and cook until the timer runs out

9. Serve and enjoy!

Nutrition: Calories 280, Fat 15 g, Carbohydrates 3 g, Protein 33 g.

45. CAJUN SHRIMP

A Perfect Classic Recipe for Fish

Easy

7 minutes

Fish Recipes

4 Servings

INGREDIENTS

¼ pound tiger shrimp, about 16-20 pieces

¼ teaspoon cayenne pepper

½ teaspoon old bay seasoning

¼ teaspoon smoked paprika

1 pinch of salt

1 tablespoon olive oil

COOKING STEPS

1. Preheat your Air Fryer to 390 degrees F in "AIR FRY" mode

2. Take a mixing bowl and add ingredients (except shrimp), mix well

3. Dip the shrimp into spice mixture and oil

4. Transfer the prepared shrimp to your cooking basket and cook for 5 minutes

5. Serve and enjoy!

Nutrition: Calories 180, Fat 2 g, Carbohydrates 5 g, Protein 23 g.

46. AIR FRIED DRAGON SHRIMP

A Perfect Classic Recipe for Fish

Easy

10 minutes

Fish Recipes

4 Servings

INGREDIENTS

1-pound raw shrimp, peeled and deveined

A ½ cup of soy sauce

2 eggs

2 tablespoons olive oil

cup yellow onion, diced

¼ cup flour

½ teaspoon red pepper, ground

½ teaspoon ginger, grounded

COOKING STEPS

1. Preheat your air fryer to 350 degrees F in "AIR FRY" mode

2. Add all the ingredients except for the shrimp to make the batter

3. Set it aside for 10 minutes

4. Dip each shrimp into the batter to coat all sides

5. Place them on the air fryer basket

6. Cook for 10 minutes

7. Serve and enjoy!

Nutrition: Calories 600, Fat 6 g, Carbohydrates 59 g, Protein 31 g.

47. MUSHROOM AND TILAPIA
A Perfect Classic Recipe for Fish

Easy

10 minutes

Fish Recipes

4 Servings

INGREDIENTS

½ cup yellow onion, sliced thin
4 ounces filets tilapia
2 tablespoons olive oil
2 cups mushroom, sliced
4 tablespoons soy sauce
2 cloves garlic, minced
tablespoon honey
tablespoons rice vinegar
and ½ teaspoon salt
1 tablespoon red chili flakes

COOKING STEPS

1. Preheat your air fryer to 350 degrees F in "AIR FRY" mode
2. Season the fish with half the salt
3. Drizzle with half the oil
4. Cook for 15 minutes
5. Take a large skillet and add remaining oil and heat it
6. Add the onion, garlic, and mushroom when it is hot
7. Cook until onions are soft
8. Stir in the soy sauce, honey, vinegar, and chili flakes
9. Simmer for 1 minute
10. Serve with mushroom sauce and enjoy!

Nutrition: Calories 300, Fat 10 g, Carbohydrates 12 g, Protein 45 g.

48. BACON-WRAPPED SHRIMP
A Perfect Classic Recipe for Fish

Easy

5 minutes

Fish Recipes

4 Servings

INGREDIENTS

1¼ pound tiger shrimp, peeled and deveined

pound bacon

COOKING STEPS

1. Preparing the Ingredients. Wrap each shrimp with a slice of bacon.

2. Refrigerate for about 20 minutes.

3. Preheat the Air fryer oven to 390 degrees F.

4. Air Frying. Arrange the shrimp in the Oven rack/basket. Place the Rack on the middle-shelf of the Air fryer oven. Cook for about 5-7 minutes.

Nutrition: Calories 70, Fat 4.5 g, Carbohydrates 0 g, Protein 7 g.

49. CRISPY PAPRIKA FISH FILLETS

A Perfect Classic Recipe for Fish

 Easy

 15 minutes

 Fish Recipes

 4 Servings

INGREDIENTS

1/2 cup seasoned breadcrumbs

tablespoon balsamic vinegar

1/2 teaspoon seasoned salt

1 teaspoon paprika

1/2 teaspoon ground black pepper

1 teaspoon celery seed

fish fillets halved

1 egg, beaten

COOKING STEPS

1. Preparing the Ingredients. Add the breadcrumbs, vinegar, salt, paprika, ground black pepper, and celery seeds to your food processor. Process for about 30 seconds.

2. Coat the fish fillets with the beaten egg; then, coat them with the breadcrumbs mixture.

3. Air Frying. Cook at 350 degrees F for about 15 minutes.

Nutrition: Calories 210, Fat 10 g, Carbohydrates 21 g, Protein 9 g.

50. AIR FRYER SALMON

A Perfect Classic Recipe for Fish

| Easy | 10 minutes | **Fish Recipes** | 2 Servings |

INGREDIENTS

½ tsp. salt
½ tsp. garlic powder
½ tsp. smoked paprika
Salmon

COOKING STEPS

1. Preparing the Ingredients. Mix spices and sprinkle onto salmon.

2. Place seasoned salmon into the Air fryer oven.

3. Air Frying. Set temperature to 400°F, and set time to 10 minutes.

Nutrition: Calories 185, Fat 11 g, Sugar 0 g, Protein 21 g.

Conclusion

I hope you enjoyed the recipes you found in this cookbook. I'm sure you've now found that Air Fryer Oven is a useful kitchen appliance that can help you prepare a variety of dishes for your family and friends. Cook delicious breakfasts, juicy meat and poultry dishes, savory seafood, vegetables, and incredible desserts. Thanks to the newest technologies, all your dishes are cooked quickly, they are tasty and useful.

In conclusion, I would like to say Thank You again for buying my cookbook. I am sure that you will return to it again and again in search of tasty and favorite recipes.

CPSIA information can be obtained
at www.ICGtesting.com
Printed in the USA
BVHW061516270521
608294BV00011B/2120

9 781802 663624